MW00939255

How To Write a Simple Book Review

It's easier than you think!

Allyson R. Abbott

ISBN-10: 1517591740
ISBN-13: 978-1517591748

Allyson R. Abbott

Contents

Allyson R. Abbott

Dedication

I would like to dedicate this book to all readers,
to all authors and all e-readers,
may you embrace literature for ever.

Allyson R. Abbott

Acknowledgements

I would like to thank all Indie authors. You share information; you support where it is needed, empathise and advise. All this is given freely to people who are your competitors for sales and the spotlight in the media. I cannot think of another industry or group of people who offer the same.

Thank you. You Rock!

Allyson R. Abbott

Introduction

'From my close observation of writers... they fall into two groups: 1) those who bleed copiously and visibly at any bad review, and 2) those who bleed copiously and secretly at any bad review.' Isaac Asimov

****

Helpful Information

For your information: if you want to buy and download e-books from Amazon and you do not have a Kindle you can download a free app for use on phones, laptops or in web browsers:

Laptops or PC's that run Windows from:
http://www.amazon.com/gp/kindle/pc/download

Smartphones/Tablets etc. from:
https://www.amazon.com/gp/digital/fiona/kcp-landing-page

Web browsers (to read from the cloud) from:
https://read.amazon.com

****

I love books and I love reading. Many years ago, in the land of paper, I would finish a novel in triumph, and if I thought it worthy, would happily pass it on to a friend or family member. I was keen to share the enjoyment of a good book and to hear their thoughts. As readers, we were not personally encouraged to write a review; that being left to the editorial sections of newspapers, publishing houses and famous people, until Amazon came along. Amazon allowed their many users to add reviews to all products; including books. Soon, book reviews came to take on a whole new meaning. Authors are now able to see first-hand how the general public reader reacts to their book. This was a great step forward, but then Amazon introduced the Kindle.

The world of books and their readers has been turned on its head. Even though it felt like cheating, or succumbing to the devil, I, like most other avid readers, moved to e-books for the convenience and the much wider variety and availability of books it offered— all at our fingertips. I still love to read a paperback, when possible, but with the new technology of being able to read using my phone, iPad or Kindle, I am never without a book and read at every opportunity.

Before I start on the subject of book reviews, I would like to explain a bit about authors and publishing, to help you appreciate their plight.

With the option of self-publishing, thousands of ordinary people (like me) are now able to write a novel or a nonfiction book, becoming an 'Independent Author' and present their book to the world, and in doing so, have bypassed the *very* selective and literary controlling publishers, who, no longer have control over what you, the reader, can read. Readers now have direct access to thousands of authors. No more gatekeepers.

There's a lot of hype about Independent 'Indie' authors and Indie publishers, and can be confusing if you're not in the know. Basically an Indie Author is someone who writes a book and has no financial backing from a Publishing House to do so. They have no contract or promised income. They need to pay for their own editing, proofreading, research, formatting, covers and publishing. An Indie Author/Publisher also then goes on to use the facilities on KDP (Amazon's Kindle Direct Publishing), which is free to use, or possibly Smashwords, (which is also free to use and distributes to other book selling organisations like Barnes and Noble, KOBO, iTunes, and many more).

If the author wants their work in a paperback, there are publishing companies like CreateSpace or LuLu.com to name two, but there are plenty more who charge for the services of publishing if the author finds the process too daunting; but the author is still independent from the big publishing houses. There are also vanity publishers, where authors can pay hundreds of pounds for publication and distribution of their books. Some of these options would not have been possible years ago, but now anyone can write a book and publish within a week or so if needed. It can be the best book you have ever read, but it could also be a stinker, with no structure or plot, poor grammar and spelling. How would you know not to buy or read that book if there is no review or feedback from other readers? The standard book blurb will always tell you it's the best book ever written; that's what it is there for.

An Indie author not only has to write the book and get it published, as they do not have any of the backing the big publishing houses offer, they are also now having to wear many different hats: author, publisher, marketer, publicity, customer services, promotion specialist. It is never ending. Their work doesn't stop with the words 'the end'. They will spend hours on social media networks, trying to be seen, or completing author profiles on different sales sites, like Amazon, to have a presence or to become a face. And, it never stops. They need to keep plugging their old works, while writing new books. Even authors who are signed up with publishers (but are not best sellers or famous), have to work hard to promote their own books.

Anita Lovett (from Anita Lovett and Associates) wrote as part of her eBook Market Review & Guide to 2015 in January of this year

> *'E-book marketing is not for the faint of heart. It's a bear, fully equipped with sharp teeth and claws. With between 600,000 to 1 million being published each year (i.e. 1,600 to 2,700 books hitting the marketplace every day), just the United States, its imperative for yours to stand out.'* (25/01/15)

Luckily, due to e-readers, all authors can now contact and interact with their readers directly, asking for opinions of their books and giving contact details. They are actually begging you to tell them your thoughts. For a lot of Indie authors, your judgement is the only feedback they can get, whether you love it or hate it. How will they ever know if it has been well received, or if they need to go back to the writing table? Publishing houses forward their authors' books to reviewers and contacts from all areas of the media, and then publish the reviews in national and international newspapers. Indie Authors do not have that backing, reach, or the means.

So, why am I going on about authors and not book reviews?

According to author Nancy Curteman in her blog on May 17, 2012, where she answered her own question of;

> *'Do Amazon reviews actually affect a book's sales?*

The answer was: 'Yes they do', according to publishers and other authors. Here's how:

- *After about ten reviews, Amazon starts including the book in "also bought" and "you might like" lists. This increases the chances of someone finding the title.*

- *After several more reviews Amazon looks at the book for spotlight positions and the newsletter. This provides a HUGE hike in sales.*

- *The number of reviews may affect Amazon sales ranking.*

- *Some websites will not consider or promote a book unless it has a number of reviews on the Amazon page.*

- *Readers may read through reviews and decide to purchase or not purchase the book based on what they read.'*

Note: As Amazon is always changing the rules, this information may be a little out of date, but the fact remains that reviews are extremely important and they will always figure in Amazons algorithms, somewhere.

Therefore, the more reviews you have, the more it will generate sales. According to Amy Gesenhues, who wrote an article on Dimensional Research website in April 2013,

"an overwhelming 90 percent of respondents who recalled reading online reviews claimed that positive online reviews influenced buying decisions, while 86 percent said buying decisions were influenced by negative online reviews."

Later in this book I will be discussing how a negative review does not necessarily stop a person from purchasing.

Any review is like a stamp of approval and social acceptance. Acknowledgement from 1000 readers (whether positive or negative) will definitely have more impact than 10 or 15 reviews. The book will be higher up in the listings on Amazon when users are searching for something similar. Believe me when I say, a review to an author is like the lights on a Christmas tree, the more there are, the more the tree will shine and get noticed. Let's just say, book reviews are important, not just to the author, but for you and other readers.

I bet, there is not one person reading this book, who can deny ever passing a book to another person to read or verbally discussing a book. If you are reading this book, you have already admitted to enjoying reading, and want to give something back, to pay the enjoyment forward. I expect you have even read reviews before buying a book! However, reviews do not appear by magic.

To clarify, when I am talking about a simple book review, I am focusing on a review or a comment of a popular fiction or a popular nonfiction book, not literary or editorial reviews, or book reports, and I have outlined the differences in 'Section 3: Type of Reviews'.

I have written this book hoping to encourage more readers to write reviews, to help readers dispel the 'fear' factor, or the 'I'm not clever enough', or hopefully the 'I can't be bothered' syndrome. Authors spend many hours, days, weeks and even years to craft a book and they need you, need all readers to rate their book and say 'thank you' or even 'I hate it' and, if possible, to say a few words why. That is all.

This book will help you to decide what to write and why. It will remove the demons and make the process simple and explain the systems. It will give examples of template reviews, to make it easier for explaining the different star ratings.

Please, if you are a reader and don't review books, read this book and think about it. That's all I ask.

Thank you for buying and reading this book, I do hope you find it helpful and that it will give you the passion and reason to leave a review.

Allyson R. Abbott

Section 1: What is a Book Review?

> '*What is in question is a kind of book reviewing which seems to be more and more popular: the loose putting down of opinions as though they were facts, and the treating of facts as though they were opinions.*'
> *Gore Vidal*

What is a book review? And why does it matter?

Wikipedia (as of 6th June 2015) says,

'*A book review is a form of literary criticism in which a book is analysed based on content, style, and merit. A book review can be a primary source opinion piece, summary review or scholarly review.*'

The term 'literary criticism' sends shivers down my spine, I don't know about you, but it takes me back to my school days, when we had to analyse a poem or a book. 'What was the author thinking when they wrote about *eyes shining bright*? How was I supposed to know? Literary criticism sounds snobbish and extremely important. However, the term criticism implies that it's preparing you for the wrongs of the text, the mistakes, indicating that the author should know better.

But, what if they don't know better? What if they are just learning their craft? Everybody has to start somewhere, and if you don't have an agent or a 'to hand' editor from a publisher, then you are on your own. Literary criticisms have their place among academic studies, but not for everyday popular fiction reviews.

Wikipedia's last statement, particularly the 'summary review' even sounds complicated.

So okay, if you have time and don't mind writing, and have practised the art of reviews, then maybe your reviews can extend to a 'summary review'. Practice will make you more confident. But nowadays, writing a review for a book does not even have to be that complicated.

The bit that stands out for me is the middle part of the quote, 'A book review can be a primary source opinion piece. And basically that is what a simple book review is. It is an opinion. It is your opinion and can be written how you like, as long or as short as you like. Do not think for one minute you need to be an accomplished reviewer to leave an opinion.

On Amazon you can find a list of their Top Reviewers. These reviewers do not just review books; they review everything, from a pair of scissors, to a top of the range TV and more. Sometimes they're offered the items for free, in exchange for a review. If that happens, they (and you) should state at the top of your review 'that the item was given in exchange for an honest review': note the word honest. **Please Note as from September 2015 Amazon have changed their review policy and no longer hold credence to 'honest reviews in exchange for goods (discounting books)**.

The Top Ranked reviewer today (6th June 2015) is Ali Julia from Boston, Massachusetts, USA, and she's written a total of 3349 reviews. I am only speculating here, but I should think there has to be money made from writing that many reviews (selling on the items for one), although for some people, it's just a hobby.

Amazon actively encourages reviews, because reviews generate sales. Buyers and users of Amazon are also encouraged to leave feedback if a particular review has 'been helpful' (even if you didn't purchase the item) as this gives the reviewer creditability.

Reviewers on Amazon actually have a ranking system and acknowledgements through, 'The

Hall of Fame,' for dedication to duty and the years of reviewing. Companies actively seek out top reviewers and send them products in exchange for one of their wordy reviews, knowing that it will be taken seriously by the buyers, due to having that "Top Amazon Reviewer' label assigned to the reviewer. It is prestigious and taken seriously. So, if you want to take it up seriously, there are options. However, an opinion is just as important as a fuller review.

Back to books, and the subject of book reviews.

A simple book review does not always need to be lengthy. What is wrong with a short 'I really loved this book. It was so exciting and kept me engrossed all the way through, I just couldn't put it down'. What is wrong with that simple book review? Nothing, as far as I am concerned. The book has been reviewed, the author will be happy and another possible reader will know at least one other reader liked it. There are plenty of two-worded book reviews, and they all have added value.

A prospective reader already knows the genre, has probably read the blurb, so understands basically what the book is all about. They have already noted how many reviews it has and what the rating is. Do they really need a full blown, chapter by chapter break down and the ins and outs of the plot, scenes and characters? Personally, I think that by this stage all they want to know, is it worth the money or my time reading? Think about your buying habits. What do you depend on?

There will always be an experienced or a 'requested' reviewer who will add a lot more detail; (an author often sends out a copy of their book to known reviewers to 'request' a review). These reviews are extremely valuable, but as a reader who has purchased a book, your opinion is just as important; you can say as much or as little as you want. Even if the book is a free book from Amazon, it is still regarded as purchased.

Everyone is different and we all have our own opinions, which is why I like to read reviews from all the different star categories, before I download a book. That way, I get a better feel for what to expect.

Previously I have read a book that has glowing 5 Star reviews and I struggled to finish it. I wrongly presumed if it has a 5 Star rating and the top few reviews are all 5 Star, then it has to be good, right? Not necessarily, because the top few reviews, could possibly be there because lots of users click on the 'has it been helpful', button, as mentioned previously. You do not even have to read or have bought the book to click on the 'was this review helpful to you' button.

It can be a tactic by some authors to try and keep the good five star reviews at the top, under the book description, so it's the next place you look after reading the book blurb. It's a marketing ploy, which is why I like to read a selection from the different star ratings. It always amazes me how a lot of these 'most helpful' are often the longest. That may be to try and push the others further down the page, out of view.

Amazon however, posts recent reviews on the right side of the page. It's a good idea to let your eyes wander over there, because most books get a lot of hyped up and promotion reviews upon (or even prior) to release and the most recent can be a good eye opener. You can always use the search options to just check the 2 star or 4 star sections if you wanted.

I am wandering off track a bit, but I have found some interesting information.

I need to adjust my theory that only 5 star reviews are 'the most helpful'. While doing some research, I thought I would find a popular book to check the 'most helpful' review.

I chose *Fifty Shades of Grey*, by E. L. James, which completely disproves only 5 Star reviews being at the top and that two-worded reviews are the least you can do. Make that one-word.

It just so happens, that in this case the most helpful review is a long 2 Star review by Meymoon posted on 15th April 2012; who openly admits that he/she does not like writing bad reviews, and goes on to explain his/her 2 Star rating quite eloquently.

I would just like to give you some facts about this book that I found interesting during this particular search.

According to Amazon, "*Fifty Shades of Grey* (on 6th June 2015) has had a total of **31,980** reviews and a 4.5 star rating. That is a lot of reviews! Harry Potter (Book 1), only had just over 10,400 (6th June 2015, Amazon).

Out of the **27,176** people who clicked the 'most helpful' button on a review, **26,149** have chosen Meymoon's 2 Star negative review; which is why it's at the top. I repeat; **26,149** people thought the 2 Star rating was the most helpful review in making their decision, whether to buy the book or not. However, even though thousands of people have clicked a negative review as being helpful, I don't think it has stopped them from buying the book. As Gesenhues pointed out, 86% of people were influenced by negative reviews, but it does not state how they were influenced. The negative reviews for *Fifty Shades of Grey*, are still rolling in. I don't think any tactics in the world would be able to take that review from the top.

That is astonishing. I then turned to the most recent reviews to find out if attitudes had changed. Not only were people still buying this 4.5 star book in droves; even though the top review is warning them not to waste money, the majority of reviews are 3 Star or less. It is like people are buying the book just to see how bad the book really is! Even in the 30 minutes that I took to jot down the following details, two more negative reviews came in.

Fifty Shades of Grey; the last 10 reviews as of date 6th June at 11.30pm Central Time Zone

Date	Stars	Words	1 Word Comments
6th June	1	1	Poor
6th June	3	21	
6th June	1	1	Awful
6th June	5	20	
6th June	2	54	
6th June	5	4	
5th June	4	9	
5th June	4	65	
5th June	5	36	
5th June	1	1	Boring
Average	3.1	21.5	

Information gathered from Amazon.com on 6th June 2015

This table shows that the average star rating at the time of writing this book (June 2015) is only 3.1 and the average amount of words written in those reviews was only 25.5. That, to me, is staggering. Now you have evidence that a review does not have to be wordy to be able to give an opinion of a book. I wondered if they have all read the same book when I read through the reviews. I find it entertaining. Sometimes, reading reviews is more fun than reading the actual book, but I have digressed, sorry.

A short review (even one word) is just as important and as valuable to the author as a long review. What I am trying to explain is, in our new technological age, where a person who can choose from one of the 3,599,486 e-books on Amazon (4th June 2015), download it in a few seconds and read it within a day or so, is not expected to write a full literary book review, or even a summary review. No one is expecting the average reader to write more than a hundred or so words, or go into lots of nitty-gritty detail.

Do you think an author will mind if a review has two or two thousand words? No, they won't. It's the act of getting any review that can boost sales, not necessarily the rating. Lots of short reviews have more impact on their sales and career, than a few long winded, giving it all away spoiler review, or a review that analyses their writing style in depth. I cannot imagine E. L. James berating the fact that some of her reviews are only one word long. The quantity in this case, is more important than a few longer quality reviews. A one star, one worded, review is just swallowed up in a mass of other reviews of 4-5 stars, but, it is the quantity of the reviews that keeps it in the limelight and creating the knock-on effect of all the publicity.

Here is a breakdown of the **31,980** reviews

24%	1 Star
9%	2 Star
9%	3 Star
11%	4 Star
47%	5 Star

Meaning, that only 58% of the reviews are positive reviews (only 5 Star and 4 Star reviews are classed as positive) and yet the book is still selling. It's the amount of reviews that keeps the book in the spotlight, because they generate more sales. So please remember, and there is a point to my ramblings, any review is valuable.

But we need to move on before you forget what this book is about.

If a reader reviews with 'I liked the story, but I got confused with the characters' or possibly- 'the plot was difficult to follow', that gives the author a big enough clue that they need to revisit the storyline, especially if they have more than one review stating a similar thing. You would hope that most authors have invested in a beta read or copyedit before publishing. Paid experts should have given feedback about plot confusion or character discrepancies, before it hits the shelf. Some authors perhaps may have missed that stage (preferring to save money and to do it themselves), but as a customer you have the right to expect a well written, edited, and proofread book. Your role as a reader, is to let the author know if you enjoyed the book or not and why. It's that simple.

Thus, a simple book review for Amazon or any other online bookshop does not have to be a book report or literary review/criticism. This confusion might be why many thousands of readers do not write reviews of the books they read. They may be thinking back to their old school days of book reports (used as a method by teachers to make sure that a books was read), or a literary review; used by scholars to show a depth of understanding of a piece of writing.

A simple informal book review of popular fiction is your opinion written with as little or as much detail as you want, with as many words as you want. I'm not saying that there is no need for long reviews, but I'm saying that not everyone needs to write them, or should be required to. I expect there may be people who disagree with me, but if they are authors I am sure they would still happily accept a one word review above no review. A one word 5 star review is worth hundreds of words and what author would not prefer a one word 1 star review to a 1 star review ripping the books to bits, although a few words to explain why it is a 1 star would be more helpful.

Plus you can have anonymity. On Amazon, you can have a 'reviewer' name. Therefore, the reviews you leave do not have to be in your account name. This makes them more private and you don't have to worry about people you know reading your reviews or challenging you. They are private and personal, only Amazon will know they come from your account if you use a reviewer name.

Allyson R. Abbott

Section 2: Why Review a Book?

'E-books are great for instant gratification - you see a review somewhere of a book that interests you, and you can start reading it five minutes later'. Anne Lamott

I will admit openly I have not always written reviews for books. I, like most other readers, have been a bit slow on the uptake. I worried my reviews would sound silly, not meaningful enough or I might get something wrong. In fact, I did get something wrong this week in a book review. I gave the main character a completely wrong name. Luckily, you can go into your account on Amazon, find 'your reviews' and edit it. But anyhow, I now realise how silly I was. There are so many two-worded reviews on Amazon, or short one or two liners, that I felt shamed into it. I have a degree in English, surely I can write a sentence or two about a book and at the same time, give the author a pat on the back, or a nudge in the ribs? But a review is not just about saying thank you, it really does help an author, especially a struggling Indie Author to get noticed.

Whether you read paperback books or e-books, you often rely on other people's opinions before you buy one. It might be the hype from the publishing house that's printed on the cover, or even from word of mouth. It is all a sales pitch. The majority of readers who search through Amazon, Barnes and Noble, or KOBO and other online book stores, generally check the review status of a book: how many reviews and what is the rating. Along with the book cover, it will then depend on your tastes, as to whether to make another click and delve deeper.

For the majority of this book I will be using Amazon as an example, mainly because it's the one I use and (I believe) is still the main leader of e-books sales. E-books now make up around 30% of all book sales, and Amazon has a 65% share within that category (www.Forbes.com, 15th July 2015).

There are three reasons why I think you should review a book: for other readers, for the author, and for yourself.

Please leave a review: For Other Readers

Does a reader, who is about to spend their well-earned money on a book, not deserve to have a selection of truthful opinions to help in the decision making? I say truthful, because it is a well-known fact that some authors pay for reviews, and other 'in-house' authors from the same publishing company, are encouraged to write a review for other authors. Whereas, I am not totally against paying for reviews, especially for Indie authors, because an Indie author cannot expect a person to give up a few hours of their life to review a book for someone else's gain. Amazon does not permit relatives and friends to review books (it will remove them if they know of any connection with the author), so authors have to depend on the services of strangers.

Recently, (July 2015) Amazon has started removing reviews (or not posting them) if they think the review is from someone who has a connection with the author. How they work out this connection or what algorithm they are using is not being made public. It seems like an invasion of privacy to me. As an author I have made many contacts with other authors, reviewers and generally people who like books and reading. Does that make them my friends and no longer able to write a review? Surely as sensible grown adults, we are capable of writing an unbiased review?

So, where do they get reviews from? How do Indie authors get their books seen and reviewed?

Paying for someone's time to read your book and write an honest opinion is fine by me. Publishing houses send books to newspaper, magazine, and journal reviewers, who are being paid to read and write about them, and they rely on them to publish the results, I fail to see the difference. Amazon disagrees and will remove reviews if they suspect any financial gain has been made. They do allow free copies of books to be given out for 'honest' review purposes, but the reviewer (not a friend or family) needs to state that in their review. Luckily, there are book reviewers who are happy to exchange a review for a book, but are under high demand, due to the amount of books published daily. **Please Note as from September 2015 Amazon have changed their review policy and no longer hold credence to 'honest reviews in exchange for goods (discounting books). However, they still do not like any connection between the reviewer and the author, therefore to make your review safe, it may be wiser to state that you received the book through a giveaway.**

What I do object to, are the unscrupulous authors who request and pay for 5 star reviews. Sometimes even writing the review themselves and getting others to post it. Desperate I think. That is unforgivable and although Amazon does it's best to weed them out, it will be hard to stop them altogether.

Therefore, readers like you rely on other true readers to be honest and to give an 'unpaid and unasked for' honest review. And it can make a difference.

So please help other readers and let them know what the book is really like and leave a review.

Please leave a review: For The Author

For an author, writing a book and not getting feedback, is like handing in your homework and it never getting marked.

We all crave feedback and acknowledgement of our efforts. If you cook a meal for your friends or family, they say thank you. You leave a tip at a restaurant for good service or food. You may tip a taxi driver, or buy a barmaid or barman a drink. You might even tip a valet or a porter. All of these examples are for people, who are getting paid at least the minimum wage for doing the job in the first place.

An Indie author's income comes from the books that are sold. The common (and usually expected) selling price is either 99p, or it's free. Yes free. Can you imagine slogging your guts out for months on a piece of work, then giving it away for free, time and time again? It is heart-breaking. However, I will admit honestly that most of my fiction books on my Kindle are free books, but I justify this to myself by making sure I leave a review once finished.

The only reason an author gives away a free book is to hope that they may gain reviews or that the reader will enjoy the book and buy another in the same series or collection.

A book can take months or years to write, from the moment of conception, through the writing, reviews, rewrites, edits, proofreading, formatting to finally publishing it. Hundreds of hours on one book, this in the end could be given away for free! Sounds crazy to me, but that's what happens. They write for the love of writing and for telling a story, or maybe for helping or offering advice.

But, if they don't get reviews, if the reader doesn't write a review, say thank you, give a written tip of thanks, then it is all for nothing. Even if you hate the book, or did not finish it because the spelling, formatting, or grammar, was so bad you took it to a charity shop, let the author know. How can they ever improve their craft of writing, if they never get feedback?

Apart from being a 'tip' to the author, whether a good or bad review, it will help the author in the long term to develop their skills. The reader is sharing their views and opinions and putting forward a sales or warning pitch. Letting other readers know how great it was, or warning them of the poor storyline or mistakes. Helping them to make up their minds, whether it is worth investing time or money into its purchase. It helps the author (and other readers) to determine its worth.

An author can receive reviews through different means, from requesting a review in exchange for a free book (or payment), a peer review (asking another author to swap reviews), a full editorial review (which usually costs a lot of money) or the customer review. Guess which one is more valuable to the author? You've got it, your review. The customer who went out of their way, gave up their time to read the book and then told them what they thought of it.

I would like to ask you a few questions to think about. When you download a free book, or even pay 99p or 9.99 for one, do you ever check to see who the publisher is? Would you know if the author is an Indie or has a contract with a publishing house? Have you ever checked to see if a book you have read or are reading was written by an Indie author?

Until I became aware of the Indie movement within authoring a book, I just presumed that the book I was reading was just another published author. I had no idea that it may have been a debut Indie author, or a bestselling author. We all find authors that we like and then read more of their books. If we can't find another book by the author, we move on to another author. It never occurred to me that it may be the case that it was the author's first and only book and others would be on the way, but it may take time.

I am not bashing 'published authors', what I am trying to do is to make you, the reader, realise that Indie authors write some great books and it is sometimes hard to pick them out from the crowd. I just think they deserve a little more recognition for all their efforts. All books though, should deserve some sort of comment.

So please for the Author's sake, leave a review.

Please leave a review: For Yourself

So, you've been reading a free book, or you may have paid good money for it, and now you have just got to the end. As you have bothered to finish it, you must have thought it was worth your time to read it. It was entertaining. Maybe it was funny and had you laughing out loud or giggling, possibly it made you scared or was sad and you shed a tear or two. Or it helped you solve a problem. You may have an invested interest in the book, or it promotes a belief, or has information about a hobby or sport that you participate in.

What do you do when you finish a book? Do you sit for a few minutes, contemplating it? Or are you smiling and grateful it was a happy ending? Do you share the information with friends on Facebook? Do you ring a friend and say, 'I have just read a great book, you must read it'! Do you leave it lying around, so you can talk about it with your next visitor? Or do you just put it on a shelf or in a bag for the charity shop?

You could reward yourself for your accomplishment of reading and completing a book, by sharing the information, thanking the author by leaving a review, and possibly making new friends by using and sharing on the Goodreads website or Facebook. There are lots of groups on Facebook where readers share reviews and feedback or discuss books. It will give you closure from the reading process and the book. You will have a feel good factor, for helping the author and for helping other readers, as well as helping to make a difference to its rankings on Amazon and other sites. Even if you did not buy the book from Amazon, you can still leave a review, as long as you have an account and have made at least one purchase.

But let me presume you have read it on a Kindle, which makes it easier for you, because the review page pops up. You could just take two minutes to write a short review. It will still help give you closure, it will help you to put the book into perspective and it will make you feel better about yourself. You should get an email from Amazon, thanking you for the review. It sometimes takes a day or two to show on the site. I prefer to use the website directly, that way I know the review is being listed. I have had reviews from my Kindle go astray. It does take longer, but I don't mind. The author has taken the trouble to entertain me, so I am happy to tip.

Please, for your own sanity, remove the book from your mind, help others and write a review.

NOTE. If you are not aware of the Goodreads website, it's a place where anyone who reads can list all their books (read, wanting to read, or reading list), whether they actually have them or not. You can share information with other readers, join different groups and enter lots of giveaway competitions. If you like reading, and would like to get to know authors or help them by reviewing books, that is the place to go. I don't think one author would turn down a review in exchange for a free copy of a book, as long as you are honest with your review and do not feel obliged to up the stars because the book was a gift.

Section 3: Type of Reviews

'I love a modern suit paired with a polo or cotton T-shirt... and then paired with leather sneakers, or cashmere joggers with a tailored blazer and a sleeveless puffer vest to get the ultimate informal and formal combination.' Brunello Cucinelli

As mentioned previously, there are different types of book review. I thought I would just clarify the difference and where they would get used, but if you know, then please jump to the next section on tips for review writing.

If you can remember your school days, then you too will remember book reports for English Literature, where every author had a second meaning to every line written, and as students it was your job to find out what it was. If, like me, you went on to higher education, then book reviews took on a whole new meaning. They became Literary Reviews or Critiques, and you actually had to read the books or articles, understand them, and quote meaningfully from them, through a correctly formatted, precisely referenced and quoted, and all within a certain word counted report or essay. It sort of took the fun out of reading.

The good news now is, that being a thoroughly educated and/or independent person, you can choose how you want to review a book. If you prefer a formal, template report, then that's great. If you want to do a full analysis, then feel free to go ahead. But, if you just want to write a few words, a few sentences and quick summary, then that is just as good and as meaningful. Your opinion counts, so let it be heard.

I actually do read quite a few reviews on Amazon, and I often get bored or stop halfway through a long-winded re-tell of the plot, character flaws, etc., and stuff that I don't really want to know. What I want to know, in a nutshell, is the book worth reading? Did you enjoy it? If so why? I do not want a re-hash of all the blurb and hype, thank you very much. Just your opinion!

If you have experience of writing literary reviews through college or university, then you may feel that this type of review holds more value and allows more detail. You may like evaluating the novel or nonfiction book and passing on your thoughts or analysing the data and facts to give your own interpretation of the evidence. These types of review are often deep and meaningful and hold no bars or give a second thought to ripping a book apart and dissecting every sentence. At the end of the day, you may have spent hours on writing and perfecting this review, and if for study purpose, then good on you, but for a popular fiction or nonfiction book, read for pleasure, I think it would be a waste. However, there are authors who hold their books in high esteem or authors of good literary fiction would probably love to have a full literary review of their work. It gives it kudos, makes it stand out from the crowd, and believe me the e-book shelves are jam packed so any arrow that says 'Pick Me! Pick Me!' is welcome.

Formal: Literary Reviews/Criticisms or Editorial Reviews

With a literary review, there is no worry about giving the ending away or revealing the plot. The whole point is to tell interested parties if the plot works or if the author has done his job properly. If it has rave editorial reviews, people will read it, no matter if they know the ending. People still buy the classics, Pride and Prejudice, Great Expectations and Jekyll and Hyde, to name a few (and even watch the films), even though they know the ending. It's the actual work that is attractive, the words and how they are written, not the ending.

In the end, a long editorial review is still only one person's opinion, in balance against the rest. And, if anyone does actually read it all through, they are still looking for the answer to the question: Is it a good book to read?

If you have the time and want to write a long review or critique, then that's great, but just remember to answer that question.

For a Literary review you will need to:

- Have thoroughly read and understood the book.
- Be confident in your opinion and facts (having other evidence to back it up if necessary).

- Have a focus and a point that you want to make and keep that as a clear target.
- Introduce, discuss and summarise.
- Use precise and particular language, which is grammar perfect and free of spelling errors. A Literary review is often seen as a formal review, poor English will detract from the value and integrity of the report.

Although literary reviews are used for more academia work, if you feel confident and want to use the structure in reviewing a popular fiction or nonfiction book, then do it. It is your review and you won't get marked on it.

Semi-Formal: Book Report

A book report is halfway between a literary review and a book review. They are used mostly in schools to help students learn a particular structure for analysing or giving information about a book. They usually start with all the formal information about the book, then includes a short summary of the theme or plot, may mention certain characters or place, you can impose you own thoughts and reflections. Although a book report is not necessarily a review, you could use the simple structure and template your own method and then expand it into a chattier format.

For example, a true book report (according to www.Infoplease.com) would need to contain:

- **Title** (underlined)/Author, Publication Information, Publisher, year, number of pages, Genre, a brief (1-2 sentences) introduction to the book and the report/review.
- **The Body** would contain: two sections.
  - The first explaining what the book is about and the author's theme or purpose (especially if it's a nonfiction book), you can include information about who tells the story, major events, the main characters, the tone or mood. As with most non editorial

reviews, it is important not to give away secrets or the ending.

- o This second section of the body is where you have a chance to write your own considerations and opinions and whether you thought the author achieved what they set out to do. Was the writing effective, or difficult to follow or understand? What were the strengths of the book, or the bits that did not work? For nonfiction: Was the author qualified or experienced enough to write about the subject? Do you agree with what was said? Don't forget to say if the book was interesting or not. Did it capture your imagination or send you to sleep? Would you recommend it to your friends or family?

- **Summary/conclusion**:
  - o This just needs a brief paragraph that puts all your thoughts into one or two sentences, emphasising your lasting impression, and recommendations as to who you think might enjoy the book.

Although a semi-formal structure, you could use the basics to create a plan for reviewing a book. There are some bits you would not need to use, in the first section, and you could just make it chatty and shorter.

Informal: Book Review

According to Stephen Hyse from Indie Unlimited (16/8/2012)

> *'In the hierarchy of reviews, a reader review is quite like one person recommending his or her doctor to another person.'*

You can't get more informal than that! A first glance it makes it seem like a book review has little worth or a place in the system. However, this is totally untrue. Later in the same article Hyse admits that

> *'Since the reader represents an author's customer base, these (*reviews*) have the potential to be very valuable'.*

Of course they are valuable. They may not have the kudos of a literary review, or the common structure of a book report, but a book review from a customer definitely has value. There are hardly any rules about writing a book review, but obviously if you want it to be taken seriously then you should not be rude and insulting. You can write as much or as little as you want, but you should not give the ending away.

A Book Review is:

- An informal piece of writing, (nobody shouts at you if it contains a grammatical or spelling error).

- It has no required length (unless that particular site you are posting it to, has length stipulations).

- You generally have to give it a heading or title (one or two words will suffice).

- You may have to give it a star rating, depending on where it is posted.

- It's up to you if you talk about the plot or name of the characters, but whatever you do, do not give the ending away or spoil it for other readers.

- You can mention your favourite bit, or what you didn't like about it.

- If you find a lot of spelling and grammatical errors then say so, maybe the formatting was wrong, too much spacing, or indentations change halfway through the book.

- An author also likes to know your interpretation of the book. You may read it in a completely different way to how the author expected it to be read. But it is not compulsory to write it if you don't want to.

- You can give your general opinion. Was it good, bad, slow, interesting?

- Did it contain bad language or was it sexually explicit? Warn other readers if it does.

- Would you recommend it to others? If so who? Romance lovers? Woman? Children? People who love horses? Whoever you think, it all helps to pad out a review and give information to another possible reader.

Just by looking at the list above, you can now begin to understand how a review can be created by a few simple sentences, and the best part is you can say what you like, as long as it is truthful and constructive. Or, if you don't want to write lots, just say one word, like hundreds of other reviewers!

Allyson R. Abbott

Section 4: Tips on How to Write a Review

'In my reviews, I feel it's good to make it clear that I'm not proposing objective truth, but subjective reactions; a review should reflect the immediate experience.' Roger Ebert

I am not a review writing expert. But, I don't believe you have to be to write a review. Most authors of popular fiction, or even the authors of the thousands of nonfiction books, that have suddenly flooded the market (including this one), are not expecting a scholarly editorial review that are pages long. They are not expecting every review to be written in perfect English. They are not even demanding a lengthy review. All they would like is a response, a hint, or a few words. Even a 'thank you', would suffice. They are just normal everyday people like you and me, who are trying to achieve something.

More experienced reviewers have learnt the art of telling the good, the bad, and the ugly using

200-300 words, but if you check through the reviews of a bestselling book on Amazon, (like *Fifty Shades of Grey*) you will find a lot of reviews with anything from 1-50 words. Does the author think they are worthless? You can bet your bottom dollar (or pound) those reviews are as gratefully received as any of the long essay types. As a novice book reviewer, all you can do is to try to put your words down on paper. The more reviews you write, the more experience you gather, the more confident you will become.

To help you get started I have put a few bits of advice and information together, but remember it is your review. You will find your own style and way of writing. There is no right or wrong review. So just relax and think about a book you have just read. Try to recall a few details.

If you are not good at recalling events, names, or even the book title sometimes, like me, then if you can be bothered and want to put a little detail into a review, you can try taking notes.

I'm not sure if every e-reader has this facility, but with a Kindle you can keep notes by highlighting text or just one word through placing your finger on the screen and tapping the word 'note', when a box appears. At the end of the book you can then use the top drop down tools bar and tap 'notes' and all your notes will show on a page telling you the notes and the locations.

I have to admit, that if I didn't have this facility, then I probably wouldn't take notes. It's too distracting from the reading, to keep putting it down to pick up a pen and write. But not everyone takes notes anyway. I think the majority of readers just rely on their memory recall.

I prefer to write my review as soon after I have finished the book as possible. I use 'Notes' App on my iPhone to write my review. It's handy and always with me, so I can write it while on a bus, at work, or as a passenger in a car. I then email it to myself for spelling and grammar checks in 'Microsoft Word' before posting. This is just me and my system. You can make your own up.

If a review is longer than my normal ones, I will also use a program available on the web called Ginger, which helps check for errors, but, that is me being paranoid. I have posted reviews, Facebook posts, and Tweets, with a spelling mistake or typos, but my posts still get taken seriously. If they were full of spelling mistakes and no grammar to speak of, then maybe not as much!

What sort of things do you need to think about from the book? Once you understand this, you will probably do it automatically when you read a book from now on.

For the purpose of these tips, I am presuming that the book you have read is a popular fiction book. Nonfiction would need further consideration and I have a paragraph or two further in this section to discuss that in more detail.

Decisions to make:

- The first thing you need to decide, is this review favourable towards the book, or are you warning other readers not to buy? This will set the tone. Your star award, if any (more on this later), will already have given a clue as to your opinion.

- Is there anything in particular that you remember about the book that stands out or you feel confident about mentioning?

- Was it so enjoyable that you couldn't put it down, or did it take ages because the plot was slow and you only read it to get your money's worth?

- Was the writing too flowery with too much detail, or did it give the basics and move on?

- Would you read another book by this author, or recommend it? If so who to?

There is a lot more you could think about and use to write a book review, but this book is about removing barriers to writing a book review. So let's stick to the short and sweet for now.

Apart from the variety of one or two word reviews 'boring,' 'awful,' 'love it,' hate it' or 'thank you', you can extend it to seven words, by creating a sentence.

I really loved this book, thank you.

If you wanted to add a few more words it could become:

I really loved this book, because it was set in New Orleans.

I really loved this book, because it was set in New Orleans and it kept the city alive through the words.

I really loved this book, because it was set in New Orleans and it kept the city alive through the words. The characters were really believable and interesting.

I really loved this book, because it was set in New Orleans and it kept the city alive through the words. The characters were really believable and interesting. I could not put the book down.

I really loved this book, because it was set in New Orleans and it kept the city alive through the words. The characters were really believable and interesting. I could not put the book down and would highly recommend it.

I really loved this book, because it was set in New Orleans and it kept the city alive through the words. The characters were really believable and interesting. I could not put the book down and would highly recommend this book to anyone who knows New Orleans, or likes paranormal stories or romance.

I really loved this book, because it was set in New Orleans and it kept the city alive through the words. The characters were really believable and interesting; especially Hugo, who was really funny. I could not put the book down and would highly recommend this book to anyone who knows New Orleans, or likes paranormal stories or romance.

I really loved this book, because it was set in New Orleans and it kept the city alive through the words. The characters were really believable and interesting; especially Hugo, who was really funny and I often laughed out loud; although, I did shed a tear every now and then at the sad parts. I could not put the book down and would highly recommend this book to anyone who knows New Orleans, or likes paranormal stories or romance.

See how easy that was? It has gone from a two word book review to an eighty word review, just by adding a few more pieces of information and data. Would you consider buying that book? Would it be enough for you to even think about buying it?

Even if the prospective buyer does not make a

decision from your review, it may spark enough interest to read a few more reviews to enable a more informed decision. But either way, your review will help other readers and also the author. That extra review could move the book up into a more visible position on Amazon. You could make a difference.

Before I move on to creating a template to help with reviews, I must point out a few 'must not dos', or more of 'there is no point in doing.'

Do not waste your time:

- Summarising the book unless you intend to write a long in detail book review. It is not necessary. Readers do not want to know what is going to happen, or how it will happen.

- Revealing the ending. Never, ever do that. Or spoil the book for future readers. Even if it's romance and everyone knows a romance has a HEA (Happy Ever After) ending. Or do they? A good piece of advice is to try not to mention anything after halfway through the story. Although, on saying that, you can mention if the book has a 'cliff hanger' ending. Not what it is, but just the fact. Some readers might appreciate that information and stay away from the book.

- Swear or be insulting. The post will never get to be seen.

- Quote long passages from the book as an example. A few words or a sentence, to emphasis a point of dialogue or language, or a description, but no more.

Once you have written a few small basic reviews, you may grow in confidence and start putting in more details of the story and how it is written. You could pad it out a bit more with introducing the book and the writer.

For example:

I have just finished reading Alice in Wonderland by Lewis Carrol (whose real name was actually Charles Lutwidge Dodgson).

That is another nineteen words. Absolutely unnecessary, but it makes the review longer.

You could even add if you had read any other books by the same author and the names of the books. So, there is no need to worry about the length or what to say. Once you start writing it will all fall into place!

It is sometimes a good idea to personalise the review.

'I loved Rosie, she reminded me of my grandmother with her 'blue hair rinse and glasses perched on her nose'.

The more personal and less technical your review, keeps it in the informal section, so there will be no need to substantiate your claims. Make it any length. Perhaps you could pretend you are talking to someone and telling them about the book. Make it chatty.

If you still need inspiration or tips, go to Amazon, Goodreads, or other online book stores and read some of the reviews. Pick a book that you have read and enjoyed and check through the reviews. Then pick a book you did not like, and read the reviews for that. Most books will have at least a few 5 Star reviews with glowing reports; someone always loves the book, but beware it may be that the review has been paid for as an 'honest' review or for a stellar (outstanding) review. So always check others further down. Did your opinions differ from the other readers? I expect they did. But everyone is allowed an opinion. If we all liked the same thing, then there would only be romance or mystery books on the shelves.

But, this brings me round to writing a negative review.

I hated it, could be turned into:

I am sorry, but I did not like this book.
But why?

I am sorry, but I did not like this book, because I found the plot too confusing to follow.
Is that all?

I am sorry, but I did not like this book, because I found the plot too confusing to follow and the characters were not convincing.
What was wrong with the characters?

I am sorry, but I did not like this book, because I found the plot too confusing to follow and the characters were not convincing. Sandy, did nothing but cry all the way through the book for every reason possible, and Billy was so boring and did nothing all day and said nothing of any importance, I don't know how he managed to make so many friends.
Okay, thank you for your review, is there anything else?

I am sorry, but I did not like this book, because I found the plot too confusing to follow and the characters were not convincing. Sandy did nothing but cry

all the way through the book for every reason possible, and Billy was so boring and did nothing all day and said nothing of any importance, I don't know how he managed to make so many friends. I found I still had too many questions at the end, like what happened to the dog? How did they end up in Brighton so quickly? Billy's mother played a major part in the book at the beginning, what happened to her, did she die from her injuries? I like an ending to be the end, where everything is tied up. Although the ending did surprise me! Therefore although the book has a good basic storyline and is easy to read, I cannot recommend this book.

Whatever you do, be honest (but not nasty) and do not worry about it. It is extremely important that you are honest, without being rude. If you did not enjoy the book, then say why, but as constructively as you can. In this review, I have broken a few rules and given away a bit of the plot, but nothing that tells the story or gives away the ending. The author could not really complain about a review like that. It is your opinion, you are being honest and explaining your reasons.

Sometimes it is easier if you have a simple template. For example, you could have a set of questions that you ask yourself for each book. If you set up a table in a Word document, you could fill in the facts and opinions and then when you transfer it to the full review add the conjunctions and more filler.

Basic template:

The Trumpet by Mr B Lower. Mystery Genre	
Question	**Answer**
Was the book interesting?	Yes
Did it grab my attention?	Yes
Was the plot easy to follow?	Most of it, but short chapters
Main characters that stood out?	Bob 'Bass' Black
Another question	
Another question	

My review

The Trumpet, by B. Lower, was very funny, even though it was a mystery. I really enjoyed it and found it an interesting book. It was easy to follow, but would have preferred longer chapters. I did get a bit confused in chapter 4.

Bob 'Bass' Black, was a very interesting character, with his witty wise cracks and constant demand for praise. I thought.......

If you are using a star rating system, add a column for that. You could even have more sections and star each one and work out the average for the overall star. This is only a small example to give you an idea. As you develop your writing skills and gain confidence you can add more and make it as complex as you like. I would suggest creating a folder and saving all your reviews in one place with the book name/author as the title. You never know when they might come in handy.

Star graded template:

The Trumpet by Mr B Lower :Mystery Genre			
Section	Question	Answer	Stars
General	Was the book interesting?	Yes	4
	Did it grab my attention?	Yes	4
	Was the actual writing good? Mistakes?		4
Theme/plot	Was the plot easy to follow?	Most of it.	3
	Did the author craft a good plot?		5
	Was there a main theme?		3
Characters	Main characters that stood out	Bob 'Bass' Black	5
	Another question		3
	Another question		3
Recommend			4
		Total / 10	3.8

The Trumpet, by B. Lower, was very funny, even though it was a mystery. I really enjoyed it and found it an interesting book. It was easy to follow although I did get a bit confused in Chapter 4.Bob 'Bass' Black, was a very interesting character, with his witty wise cracks and constant demand for praise. I thought.......

The overall total was 38 points divided by 10 gives 3.8. Most review sites do not allow half stars, so at 3.8 you then decide it if was a 3 Star or a 4 Star book.

At the end of most e-books there is usually a request for the reader to leave a review, usually with a star system (1-5), 1 being very bad and 5 being very good. It could possibly take as little as one minute to leave a review, and yet few people actually do. I can remember reading an article on giving away your book for free to hopefully encourage more readers and hence, reviews, but the article warned only to expect about 2 reviews for every hundred books given away. One of my short stories was downloaded for free 543 times on one website and I only received two reviews; that is a poor return for a lot of work. Hopefully, you can begin to understand why Indie Authors ask friends, relatives and pay for reviews. If you give books away and hardly receive reviews, then what chance do you have selling them and expecting reviews?

Amazon has its own star rating system which is:

1 Star: *I hated it*

2 Star: *I didn't like it*

3 Star: *It's OK*

4 Star: *I like it*

5 Star: *I loved it*

Sounds simple, but when you actually come to 'Star' a book it gets harder, especially if it's in the middle. Nobody likes to give a negative review; especially peer reviews, but you need to be honest. You cannot point out lots of bad things about a book and then give it four stars. Having a grading system helps you to justify your rating (if you feel you need to justify it).

You could have your own easy to read grading system. Decide what would make you rate a book 5 Star, then think about a 1 Star and gradually fill in the in between grades. The good thing about a grading system or chart is that it offers you a good reason as to why you only gave 2 or 3 stars if ever asked.

> *'I can only give 2 stars because according to my grading system there were too many errors, and the characters were not well developed enough to give it 3 stars. Sorry.'*

It is giving a reason and you are explaining that you have a structure that you work to.

Let me explain further and create a grading system.

You can add your own standards and you will probably change or add to them as you do more reviews. This table below is just a basic example, but it gives you an idea of how to grade.

Grading System

Explanation and Reasoning	Star
This book kept me hooked right until the end. I could not put it down. The characters felt real and I understood their actions. The plot had lots of twists and turns, but the author was able to make sure the reader could follow. The blurb and the cover were both attention grabbing and suitable for a book of that genre. The author's writing was descriptive; was showing, not telling. Fast paced and easy to read, only a little bit of technical language. Only a couple or misspelt words or typo's. Would highly recommend this book to thriller lovers, anyone who reads the likes of Harlan Coben or Lee Child (or any other authors).	5

Explanation and Reasoning	Star
I finished the book fairly quickly and was kept interested to the end. Plot was good and paced well for the storyline. Good realistic characters and I could relate to most of them. The story did dry up a little in the middle, but the characters pulled it through. A few spelling and grammatical mistakes. Blurb and cover good. Would recommend this book to other readers.	4

Explanation and Reasoning	Star
I finished the book, but struggled. Storyline was good, but the scenes did not flow very well. Characters were okay, but nothing great Needs a good edit. Would only recommend to people who do not mind swearing or foul language. Book cover was good. Blurb really bad and did not warn about the language.	3

Explanation and Reasoning	Star
I finished the book, struggled to understand the plot and the ending. A good story, but very slow and wordy. Characters were not well enough developed, with lots of missing detail. Had potential, but the author missed chances to bring the reader in. Too many grammatical errors and the formatting was annoying. Blurb was good, but cover did not reflect the genre (misleading).	2

Explanation and Reasoning	Star
I have finished reading the book , but: The plot did not work and the characters were boring. The pace was too slow. There was too much talking and not enough action. There were lots of spelling errors and grammatical errors. Distracted from the reading. I could not recommend this book to anyone. The cover was deceiving. The book did not live up to the blurb.	1

Having your own grading system would help if you cannot make your mind up about what star to rate a book. The template makes it easier for you to look at and get an overall picture. It does make life simpler, but I am all for writing on the hoof and making a decision there and then. This template is only using basic examples. But you might have similar questions in each section, but reworded to explain the difference.

For example:

5 Star statement: *Only one or two spelling mistakes or typos. No grammar issues*

4 Star statement: *Quite a few spelling mistakes and some grammar issues*

3 Star statement: *Too many spelling mistakes and grammar issues*

2 Star statement: *The amount of spelling and grammar issues distracted me from the book*

1 Star statement: *There were so many mistakes I had trouble understanding it on occasions*

Did Not Finish: *Too many mistakes to be able to read and enjoy the book*

You could create your own list of standardised

questions for different elements like plot, pace, characters, etc. That would make it easier and quicker to make a decision and write a review, especially as you will have the facts in front of you.

Nonfiction Book Reviews

A nonfiction book, like this one, serves a different purpose from a fiction book, so there are different considerations to be taken into account when writing a nonfiction review. I quite like to read an autobiography, although they can sometimes read like fiction. I also read travel books and recipe books. It took me a while to get to grips with writing a review for a nonfiction book, and I think this was due to my attitude to reading them. They were purchased, not so much for entertainment or leisure, but for a purpose, therefore they were just doing what they were supposed to do. It was not until the Indie author/self-publishing revolution, when the book market became awash with hundreds and thousands more recipe books and travel books etc., that I realised that the authors of these books warrant feedback as well. I came to this conclusion after encountering some really badly formatted books with errors in recipes and information.

My first thought was to get in touch with the

authors to let them know, but then I also decided to write and leave a review to make sure that other readers were aware of the poor quality. One book that I read was so bad that I emailed the author first and suggested that maybe he should get the book re-edited and proofread and I prepared him for my 2-star review. The author asked me not to leave the review. He did not say he was going to make any changes or appear shocked at my email. As far as I am aware the book has never been changed or amended. That makes me angry, because other buyers are getting a poorly written book and readers deserve better. All the reviews before mine failed to mention mentioned the mistakes or the crude formatting, which makes me wonder how many were paid for or how many friends the author has.

Sometimes, when reading from my Kindle I use the **Note** facility to tag spelling and grammar issues. If it's only one or two, then I don't bother writing about them in the review, but if there are lots, then I mention it or email the author directly. There are usually contact details somewhere in the book. They have always appreciated my emails and thanked me. If it was my book, I would want to know if there was a mistake in it.

It actually happened to me a couple of months ago. I asked a Goodreads reviewer if she would review one of my books. I was horrified when she gave me heads up of the review she was about to post, telling me that it was full of grammatical and punctuation mistakes. I was even more upset to find out it was true. Even though it had received 10 5 star reviews, no one else had mentioned it. I pulled the book and sent it back to be re-edited. I was very grateful for the reviewer for pointing it out to me. And I employed a new editor.

Section 5: Then What?

'Life is a very orderly thing, but in fiction there is a huge liberation and freedom. I can do what I like. There's nothing that says I can't write a page of full stops. There is no 'should' involved, although you wouldn't know that from literary reviews and critics.'
Kate Atkinson

Okay, so you may be convinced that writing a review is not that bad, in fact it is a good idea, because you can have closure, give an opinion and help the author and other readers at the same time. Hopefully, you will get to enjoy writing reviews, gain in confidence and feel able to go a step further. Maybe you will grow into a review geek, and want to share your reviews, blog about your reviews, get paid to review or possibly have such a following and respect for your reviews that authors actually contact you directly and ask for you to do a review of their book. I often pay for reviews, but use them for my own use as feedback on my writing. They do not necessarily get published anywhere. How else am I going to find out if my book is good or not?

This may seem really farfetched, but remember there are over two thousand e-books published every day (according to Anita Lovett, Chapter 1). That is a lot of authors jockeying for position and it has been proven that visibility improves as reviews increase. The best route to the top of a genre section on Amazon is either to have a lot of sales or a lot of reviews, usually one comes with the other, but reviews can come without the sales. Having them both is a sure winner, but people usually do not buy a book, if there is not a review. It's a chicken and egg situation. So authors are forced to find reviews by other means. Authors published by publishing houses have a head start. Indie authors need to find reviews through other means, such as scouring the web for reviewer's web pages, checking out Facebook groups and ask for a review, join groups that swap reviews, or ask its members to review your book. So, let me assure you, if you did become confident and even managed to start a blog or a website sharing your reviews, you will be in demand.

You can earn money as a book reviewer through www.fiverr.com or www.peopleperhour.com, they have lots of people offering their services, either just to review for the author, or to review and post on a website like Amazon, Goodreads, Facebook groups, or Barnes and Noble, or to on their own Facebook page or blog/website. As I have stated before, Amazon does not endorse paying for a review, so make sure it is all done discreetly and you are not influenced by the payment to give a 5 star review. You are being paid to write an honest review, not to sell your soul. There is no benefit financially for you to lie. Write an honest review and if it is 3 or less stars then contact the author first and ask if they still want it posted on the web. I am happy to get honest reviews for my books and I do not expect everyone to like my stories; everyone is different. As long as the reviewer is not nasty or rude, it is a review and it counts. There are the less scrupulous authors and reviewers who come to an agreement and no reading is done. The author provides the 5 star review they want posted and the reviewer is happy to take the money for no work.

On Amazon you do not need to have purchased a book from them to enable you to post a review. Most authors who want a review are happy to give a free copy away, but you must always declare if the book was a gift in return for a review. **Please Note as from**

September 2015 Amazon have changed their review policy and no longer hold credence to 'honest reviews in exchange for goods (discounting books). However, they still do not like any connection between the reviewer and the author, therefore to make your review safe, it may be wiser to state that you received the book through a giveaway.

On Fiverr or PPH, you can outline what sort of review you will do and how long it will be and charge more if the customer wants more. You can also stipulate what sort of books you will review and what you do not touch. There would be no point in trying to review a vampire story, if you really dislike vampires. You would have a negative vibe from the start. You may also want to draw the line at erotica, children's books, religious, or nonfiction.

The best way to learn about reviews is to actually see them and understand how they are written. Online book stores are not the only places that have reviews of books, there are hundreds of book bloggers out there, as well as book reviewers (personal and linked to organisations). There are a lot of websites that offer to promote books for authors and they often review the books as well and always need reviewers on their books. As I like books, I am a member of quite a few Facebook groups where authors promote their books as well as reviewers sharing their opinions. Every day you can find lots of authors who offer their books for free in exchange for an honest review. There are also many giveaway competitions, where groups, authors, reviewers or promoters are lobbying for more likes or followers and asking for you to share their pages. I am sure there must be over a hundred Facebook groups that are linked to books / reading / reviewing or giveaways.

The world is your oyster, or so they say. All you need to do is to start reviewing books and then perfect your art, through experience. There is no harm in finding a reviewer whose style you like and copy the style, but obviously not their words.

Goodreads and LibraryThing are two more places where you can find reviews on thousands of books, and if you like reading I would suggest you join. It's a great way to interact with other book lovers. Or maybe, you just prefer to read a book when you come across it and are not interested in interacting with a larger community.

To give you a helping hand, I have trawled the

web and come up with some websites that are either blogging about books, or reviewing. I have also listed some of the Facebook groups, where you can find free books or possibly find an author and approach asking to review their book.

Don't forget, the first book you can practice with is this one. Answer these questions and then decide on a star rating:

- Have you learnt anything from this book?

- If you have never written a review, do you now feel confident to do so?

- Was there enough information and evidence to help you understand the need for more book reviews?

- Would you recommend this book to others?

I thank you in advance.

I also thank you on behalf of all the authors whose books you might be writing a review for in the future. As an author, I can empathise with their plight.

Section 6: Book Bloggers and Reviewers

'Prolonged, indiscriminate reviewing of books is a quite exceptionally thankless, irritating and exhausting job. It not only involves praising trash but constantly inventing reactions towards books about which one has no spontaneous feeling whatever.'
George Orwell

Book Bloggers/Reviewers and Facebook groups and pages

This section gives lots of links and websites that will help you to understand about different reviews and writing. However, as mentioned in a previous chapter, Amazon, may frown upon any regular connections with authors and they do not like 'paid' reviews. In theory, even giving a book is a payment.

Book Bloggers as listed on

http://www.cision.com/uk/social-media-index/literature-blogs-uk-top-10/

last updated on 20/5/2015

1) The Book Smugglers

2) Playing by the book

3) Savidge Reads

4) An Awfully Big Blog Adventure

5) Book Chick City

6) Girls Heart Books

7) Wondrous Reads

8) Mr Ripleys Enchanted Books

9) Vulpes Libris

10) One More Page

There are literally hundreds more blogs on the web, and I can't log them all, but do a Google or Bing search on book blogs or book bloggers. Check out the different styles. Some book bloggers only focus on one genre, like children's books or YA (Young Adult), but others could blog about any genre or issues relating to books.

A Blogger may not review a book at all. They may just blog about release dates, or new books by popular authors, but most will review the books as well. A lot of book reviewers have blogs as well, but they also post their reviews to other sites. Their interest in books and helping authors seems to be their driving force, but they soon can have a large following themselves.

There are few examples here, but if you use the URL at the top, on that webpage there is a huge table of book reviewers who review Indie Author's books. You can also see where they post their reviews.

Lots of reviewer links here:-

1) http://www.theindieview.com/indie-reviewers
2) https://carrieslager.wordpress.com/
3) http://gutreactionreviews.com/

Some Facebook Groups to check out. If you want to join a group just click on the join button, but make sure you have read the group rules first. In most groups you have to wait for one of the administrators to accept your application before you can post or interact with other members. Some groups have thousands of members.

- **Book Reviews:**
  https://www.Facebook.com/groups/14916716
  87761808/

- **Book Reviews, Blogs, and Amazon Links Promoting Group**.
  https://www.Facebook.com/groups/1592697214295201/
- **Book review and promotion**
  https://www.Facebook.com/groups/148313988694907
- **Mainly for authors but there will be lots of free books.**

Use the Facebook search facility and check the Group bar and type in 'book, reviewer, or free books, promotions, and similar words and you will find lots to keep you busy for hours.

Personal Facebook pages that encourages interaction

- https://www.Facebook.com/BookVigilanteReviews
- https://www.Facebook.com/pages/Book-Reviews-and-Promotions/1013693618646615
- https://www.Facebook.com/BookReviewsByLexi

Okay, so, this is me signing off. I hope if you have ever considered reviewing a book and never got round to it, you may now feel more confident. With the templates and grading system that I have demonstrated, you can see how easy it is to start simple and build up a review. There is a demand for reviews on a lot of reviewing web pages and directly from authors. You could start your own Facebook page or blog. Just put the word book in the title and you will start attracting readers and authors straight away. If you join a book group, just offer to review a book. Try to do it within a week and I advise starting off with a genre that you would enjoy. Aim for a hundred words or a hundred and fifty if you think you can manage it. Look at other reviews for help and tips. If you want to charge for a review, then you need to be discreet, as Amazon frowns on it and may remove your review. If you have been given a book for reviewing purposes then make sure you declare that in the first line, if possible.

Thank you again for buying and reading this book. Good luck with your book reviewing future.

Allyson R. Abbott

Section 7: Bibliography

Life is full of surprises. My understanding is, if you 'pay it forward' and help those in need, it may hopefully catch up with you when your turn arrives. A. R. Abbott

Bibliography

Isaac Asimov. BrainyQuote.com. Xplore Inc, 2015. 14 July 2015.
http://www.brainyquote.com/quotes/quotes/i/isaacasimo140877.html

Gore Vidal. BrainyQuote.com. Xplore Inc, 2015. 19 July 2015.
http://www.brainyquote.com/quotes/quotes/g/gorevidal112496.html

Anne Lamott. BrainyQuote.com. Xplore Inc, 2015. 14 July 2015.
http://www.brainyquote.com/quotes/quotes/a/annelamott573861.html

Brunello Cucinelli. BrainyQuote.com. Xplore Inc, 2015. 14 July 2015.
http://www.brainyquote.com/quotes/quotes/b/brunellocu694990.html

Roger Ebert. BrainyQuote.com. Xplore Inc, 2015. 14 July 2015.
http://www.brainyquote.com/quotes/quotes/r/roge rebert543471.html

Kate Atkinson. BrainyQuote.com. Xplore Inc, 2015. 14 July 2015.
http://www.brainyquote.com/quotes/quotes/k/kate atkins503525.html

Orwell, George:

http://thinkexist.com/quotation/prolonged-indiscriminate_reviewing_of_books_is_a/261102.html

Curteman, Nancy

https://nancycurteman.wordpress.com/2012/05/17/how-to-write-a-book-review-on-amazon/

Lovett, Anita.

http://anitalovett.com/2015/01/25/how-do-i-get-ebook-reviews/

Accessed on 19th July 2015

http://marketingland.com/survey-customers-more-frustrated-by-how-long-it-takes-to-resolve-a-customer-service-issue-than-the-resolution-38756

Section 8: References

Accessed on 4th June 2015

http://www.ttms.org/say_about_a_book/whats_a_book_review.htm

http://www.nytimes.com/2012/08/26/business/book-reviewers-for-hire-meet-a-demand-for-online-raves.html?_r=1

http://www.quora.com/What-percentage-of-buyers-write-reviews-on-Amazon

http://www.theguardian.com/books/2011/feb/04/research-male-writers-dominate-books-world

http://www.booktrust.org.uk/books/teenagers/writing-tips/tips-for-writing-book-reviews/

http://www.scribendi.com/advice/how_to_write_a_book_review.en.html

Accessed on 5th June 2015

http://www.writing-world.com/freelance/asenjo.shtml

http://www.infoplease.com/homework/wsbookreporths.htm

http://www.indiesunlimited.com/2012/08/16/encore-three-types-of-reviews/

http://www.amazon.com/forum/top%20reviewers?
encoding=UTF8&cdForum=Fx2Z5LRXMSUDQH2
&cdThread=Tx1IUW7NNQ6SBGD

Accessed on 6th June 2015

http://anitalovett.com/2015/01/25/how-do-i-get-ebook-reviews/

http://www.amazon.com/Fifty-Shades-Grey-E-James-ebook/product-reviews/B007L3BMGA/ref=cm_cr_dp_see_all_btm
?ie=UTF8&showViewpoints=1&sortBy=bySubmissi
onDateDescending

Accessed on 7th June 2015

http://thinkexist.com/quotation/prolonged-indiscriminate_reviewing_of_books_is_a/261102.htm
l

https://carrieslager.wordpress.com/

http://www.theindieview.com/indie-reviewers/

http://gutreactionreviews.com/

Accessed n 14th July 2015

http://www.digitalbookworld.com/2014/is-apple-now-the-no-2-ebook-retailer-in-the-u-s/

http://www.forbes.com/sites/jeffbercovici/2014/02
/10/amazon-vs-book-publishers-by-the-numbers/

https://hbr.org/2012/03/bad-reviews-can-boost-sales-heres-why

http://www.slate.com/articles/arts/culturebox/2003
/09/book_report.html

About Allyson

Thank you for buying my book and reading as far as this. As I am fairly new at being an author, I am always humbled when someone reads my words.

Every book I write takes many hours and days to put together, and get it to the publishing stage. I still get a thrill when I see my books on Amazon and other eBook stores. It was only after publishing my second romance book that I realised, although I was building a following for my books, those readers were not leaving reviews. It took me until after my third book to realise that reviews are the most important factor in an author's success, providing crucial feedback, helping with sales and increasing exposure.

I talked to friends and family and asked a lot of other people who read lots of books, if they left reviews when they had finished a book, as well as, if they understood the difference between an Indie Author and a Contracted Author. I was shocked to find that I was the only person within my circle of friends and family that left reviews. The most common answer was *'I have no idea where to start'* and I was very surprised to discover that most had little, or no idea about the Indie Author movement, even though they knew I wrote books and I am an independent author. I have to admit that, as I travel a lot, it was not something we sat down at the table to discuss, but I realised that there must also be a lot more people out there who do not know how to write a review, or understand the importance of reviews for authors. I certainly didn't until I became an author.

So, to help put a tiny bit of the 'world to rights', where I can, I dedicated some hours, days and weeks to write and publish this book. It is only my opinion and it is not a bible for review writing, but it may just help or encourage more readers to write reviews and therefore help authors to develop and gain a presence in a very competitive area.

I am happy to discuss this, or any of my other books, or answer questions.

If you enjoyed this book would you please take a moment to write a review of it so that other readers can enjoy it too? Just a couple of sentences. It would mean a lot to me.

Please feel free to contact me

With best regards

Allyson R. Abbott

Other books by Allyson R. Abbott

<u>Silver Night Romance</u>
<u>Quick Reads</u>

Countdown to Love
Salsa or Die
An English Rose

<u>Silver Years Romance</u>
<u>Novellas</u>

Touching Ed
Abby and Ed Series Book 1

Managing Ed
Abby and Ed Series Book 2

Goodbye, Hello

Allyson R. Abbott

Contacts

I can be contacted via email and always appreciate feedback or comments about my books. I will reply to all emails but please be patient as I write while travelling and don't always have access to the Internet.

My email address is
Allyson.Abbott@hotmail.com
in addition you can follow me on:-

My Blog:
http://AllysonRAbbott.blogspot.com

Goodreads:
http://www.goodreads.com/AllysonRAbbott

Facebook:
https://www.facebook.com/AllysonRAbbott

Twitter:
https://twitter.com/AllysonRAbbott

LinkedIn:
http://www.linkedin.com/in/AllysonRAbbott

Links to all of these, as well as the latest information about my books and more can be found on my web site:

http://www.AllysonRAbbott.com